Too much with the hearts?

TRANSWORLD PUBLISHERS 61–63 Uxbridge Road, London W5 5SA
A Random House Group Company www.transworldbooks.co.uk

First published in Great Britain in 2013 by Bantam Press
an imprint of Transworld Publishers

A CIP catalogue record for this book is available from the British Library.

ISBN 9780593071601

Addresses for Random House Group Ltd companies outside the UK can be found at:
www.randomhouse.co.uk The Random House Group Ltd Reg. No. 954009

Printed and bound in China

2 4 6 8 10 9 7 5 3 1

Love is me saying it again on this page.

Waldo Pancake

I love you so much
that I went into a
shop and bought
you a little book
about it.

They should make a film about our life together. Minus the watching-TV-on-the-sofa-most-of-the-time bit.

Me

You

society's
pressures

You can fold
my corner
over any
time.

I love it when you use my pockets as a bin for your chocolate wrappers etc.

Absence makes the choosing what to watch on TV much easier.

Let's paint the town red.

I've just thought this through and realized how much hassle it'd be.

When we have a hug,
I always imagine you're
doing one of those looks
over my shoulder like in
a soap opera, hence me
always hugging you when
we're between two mirrors.

You bring
out the
schmaltz
in me.

You had whatev you said

ne at
er it was
.

Would it be weird if I had you stuffed if you died first?

I'm not saying I love your snoring, but the fact that it doesn't make me want to strangle you speaks volumes.

You know when you see
each other's eyes and
and it makes you want

That

a couple looking into

iggling and canoodling

o be sick?

's us.

You bring out the best in me*

*worst might also be brought out.

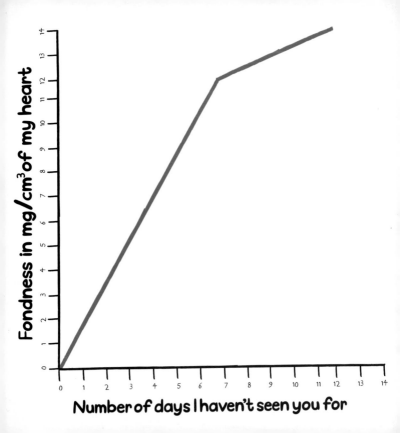

no pressure
there then ———————→

You're my reason for li♥ing.

How ironic would it be if you threw this book at me during a row.

What's with hearts not being heart shaped?

You are
great

re the
est*

*no scientific proof of this.

I like to imagine us as a really old couple, walking along the street with our sticks, holding hands. Although we'll probably have carrier bags in our spare hands. Saying that, shopping'll be done on the internet by then, won't it. Amazing isn't it.

I've read the book*

*what you can say now when subject of love comes up.

You know how couples are always picking bits of fluff off each other's jumpers?

That's why single people are so fluffy.

I love you
even more
than

I saw one of your socks
on the floor and I felt
the same love for it
that I do for you.

How sad would it be if
I was in a charity shop
after we'd split up or
whatev and I saw this
book on the shelf.

Have you seen those little birds on nature programmes that do their nests up then dance around, trying to attract a mate?

That was me that time when I tidied up my flat at the beginning of our relationship.

LL

Imagine if 'hate' meant 'love' and vice versa. I reckon there'd be loads more people saying they loved each other.

People always say 'fall in love', which makes me think of someone falling, and how they look terrified.

You know when I'm not listening to what you're saying? That's because I'm too busy thinking about you.

Weird that if we hadn't met I'd be giving this book to someone else.

(Pretend I didn't just think that then write it down and get it printed.)

I only have
eyes for
you.
And TV.

I had a massive wave of love for you today. It's gone now.

Love is me immediately thinking you've moved whatever it is I'm loooking for.

IF I GOT LOVE TATTOOED ONTO MY FOREHEAD IN TRIBUTE TO OUR RELATIONSHIP WOULD IT BE WEIRD?

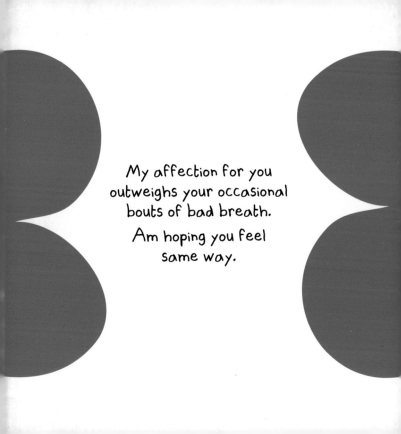

My affection for you outweighs your occasional bouts of bad breath.

Am hoping you feel same way.

Hi, this is the author. I'd just like to point out that it's me writing all this stuff, not the person who bought it for you.

You say tomato,
I go to the fridge
and get you one.

I've contemplated the whole scattering petals thing. Is that good enough for you?

Canoodle,
willoodle.

I love you
to bits.

→

eye x2   kidney x2
nose   spleen
ear x2   shoulder x2
mouth   neck
leg x2   elbow x2
arm x2   palm x2
nipple x2   bum
thumb x2   thigh x2
fingers x8   etc.
knee x2
ankle x2
heart
liver
lung x2

ve

you

My better half

→

Stick
photo of
loved
one here*

*not gonna happen.

Weird how adding poo to something makes it more lovey-dovey.

Like, 'How's my darling poopoo today?'

It just workypoos.

When I put my
arm round you,
sometimes it's
to rest my arm.

Brilliant, another person for me to worry about dying.

You know when you're talking and it's like I'm looking right through you? That's because eyes are the windows to your soul, and I'm staring right at it,

BABY.

Completely
and utterly
loved out.

Coming soon:
Hate is me
not buying
you this book.

You and
me'll
never end.